GOD OF DELIVERANCE

A STUDY OF EXODUS 1–18

JEN WILKIN

Lifeway Press® Nashville, Tennessee

EDITORIAL TEAM
LIFEWAY WOMEN PUBLISHING

Becky Loyd
Director, Lifeway Women

Tina Boesch
Manager, Lifeway Women
Bible Studies

Sarah Doss
Editorial Project Leader, Lifeway
Women Bible Studies

Elizabeth Hyndman
Content Editor

Erin Franklin
Production Editor

Lauren Ervin
Graphic Designer

Published by Lifeway Press® • © 2021 Jen Wilkin

ISBN: 978-1-0877-1325-0

Item: 005826384

Dewey Decimal Classification: 222.12
Subject Headings: BIBLE. O. T. EXODUS 1–18 / PROVIDENCE AND GOVERNMENT OF GOD / LOVE—RELIGIOUS ASPECTS

Unless otherwise indicated, all Scripture quotations are from The ESV® Bible (The Holy Bible, English Standard Version®), copyright © 2001 by Crossway, a publishing ministry of Good News Publishers. Used by permission. All rights reserved. Scripture quotations marked (NIV) are taken from the Holy Bible, New International Version®, NIV® Copyright © 1973, 1978, 1984, 2011 by Biblica, Inc.™ Used by permission of Zondervan. All rights reserved worldwide. www.zondervan.com. The "NIV" and "New International Version" are trademarks registered in the United States Patent and Trademark Office by Biblica, Inc. ™

To order additional copies of this resource, order online at www.lifeway.com; write Lifeway Christian Resources Customer Service: One Lifeway Plaza, Nashville, TN 37234-0113; fax order to 615.251.5933; or call toll-free 1.800.458.2772.

Author is represented by Wolgemuth & Associates, Inc.

Printed in the United States of America

Lifeway Women Publishing
Lifeway Resources
One Lifeway Plaza
Nashville, TN 37234

Contents

ABOUT THE AUTHOR

Jen Wilkin is an author and Bible teacher from Dallas, Texas. She has organized and led studies for women in home, church, and parachurch contexts. Her passion is to see others become articulate and committed followers of Christ, with a clear understanding of why they believe what they believe, grounded in the Word of God. Jen is the author of *Ten Words to Live By: Delighting in and Doing What God Commands*, *Women of the Word*, *None Like Him*, *In His Image* and Bible studies exploring the Sermon on the Mount and the Books of Genesis, Hebrews, and 1 Peter. You can find her at JenWilkin.net.

FOREWORD: HOW SHOULD WE APPROACH GOD'S WORD?

OUR PURPOSE

The Bible study you are about to begin will teach you an important passage of the Bible in a way that will stay with you for years to come. It will challenge you to move beyond loving God with just your heart to loving Him with your mind. It will focus on answering the question, "What does the Bible say about God?" It will aid you in the worthy task of God-discovery.

You see, the Bible is not a book about self-discovery; it is a book about God-discovery. The Bible is God's declared intent to make Himself known to us. In learning about the character of God in Scripture, we *will* experience self-discovery, but it must not be the object of our study. The object must be God Himself.

This focus changes the way we study. We look first for what a passage can teach us about the character of God, allowing self-discovery to be the by-product of God-discovery. This is a much better approach because there can be no true knowledge of self apart from knowledge of God. So when I read the account of Jonah, I see first that God is just and faithful to His Word—He is faithful to proclaim His message to Nineveh no matter what. I see second that I, by contrast (and much like Jonah), am unjust to my fellow man and unfaithful to God's Word. Thus, knowledge of God leads to true knowledge of self, which leads to repentance and transformation. So are confirmed Paul's words in Romans 12:2 that we are transformed by the renewing of our minds.

Most of us are good at loving God with our hearts. We are good at employing our emotions in our pursuit of God. But the God who commands us to love with the totality of our hearts, souls, and strength also commands us to love Him with all of our minds. Because He only commands what He also enables His children to do, it must be possible for us to love Him well with our minds or He would not command it. I know you will bring your emotions to your study of God's Word, and that is good and right. But it is your mind that I am jealous for. God intends for you to be a good student, renewing your mind and thus transforming your heart.

OUR PROCESS

Being a good student entails following good study habits. When we sit down to read, most of us like to read through a particular passage and then find a way to apply it to our everyday lives. We may read through an entire book of the Bible over a period of time, or we may jump around from place to place. I want to suggest a different approach, one that may not always yield immediate application, comfort, or peace, but one that builds over time a cumulative understanding of the message of Scripture.

READING IN CONTEXT AND REPETITIVELY

Imagine yourself receiving a letter in the mail. The envelope is handwritten, but you don't glance at the return address. Instead you tear open the envelope, flip to the second page, read two paragraphs near the bottom, and set the letter aside. Knowing that if someone bothered to send it to you, you should act on its contents in some way, you spend a few minutes trying to figure out how to respond to what the section you just read had to say. What are the odds you will be successful?

No one would read a letter this way. But this is precisely the way many of us read our Bibles. We skip past reading the "envelope"—*Who wrote this? To whom was it written? When was it written? Where was it written?*—and then try to determine the purpose of its contents from a portion of the whole. What if we took time to read the envelope? What if, after determining the context for its writing, we started at the beginning and read to the end? Wouldn't that make infinitely more sense?

In our study, we will take this approach to Scripture. We will begin by placing our text in its historical and cultural context. We will "read the envelope." Then we will read through the entire text so that we can better determine what it wants to say to us. We will read repetitively so that we might move through three critical stages of understanding: comprehension, interpretation, and application.

STAGE 1: COMPREHENSION

Remember the reading comprehension section on the SAT? Remember those long reading passages followed by questions to test your knowledge of what you had just read? The objective was to force you to read for detail. We are going to apply the same method to our study of God's Word. When we read for comprehension, we ask ourselves, *What does it say?* This is hard work. A person who *comprehends* the account of the six days of creation can tell you specifically what happened on each day. This is the first step toward being able to interpret and apply the story of creation to our lives.

STAGE 2: INTERPRETATION

While comprehension asks, *What does it say?*, interpretation asks, *What does it mean?* Once we have read a passage enough times to know what it says, we are ready to look into its meaning. A person who *interprets* the creation story can tell you why God created in a particular order or way. She is able to imply things from the text beyond what it says.

STAGE 3: APPLICATION

After doing the work to understand what the text says and what the text means, we are finally ready to ask, *How should it change me?* Here is where we draw on our God-centered perspective to ask three supporting questions:

- What does this passage teach me about God?
- How does this aspect of God's character change my view of self?
- What should I do in response?

A person who *applies* the creation story can tell us that because God creates in an orderly fashion, we, too, should live well-ordered lives. Knowledge of God gleaned through comprehension of the text and interpretation of its meaning can now be applied to my life in a way that challenges me to be different.

SOME GUIDELINES

It is vital to the learning process that you allow yourself to move through the three stages of understanding on your own, without the aid of commentaries or study notes. The first several times you read a passage, you will probably be confused. In our study together, not all the homework questions will have answers that are immediately clear to you. This is actually a good thing. If you are unsure of an answer, give it your best shot. Allow yourself to feel lost, to dwell in the "I don't know." It will make the moment of discovery stick. We'll also expand our understanding in the small-group discussion and teaching time.

Nobody likes to feel lost or confused, but it is an important step in the acquisition and retention of understanding. Because of this, I have a few guidelines to lay out for you as you go through this study.

1. **Avoid all commentaries** until *comprehension* and *interpretation* have been earnestly attempted on your own. In other words, wait to read commentaries until after you have done the homework, attended small-group time, and listened to the teaching. And then, consult commentaries you can trust. Ask a pastor or Bible teacher at your church for suggested authors. I used the following commentaries in creating this study: *Exodus: an Exegetical and Theological Exposition of Holy Scripture* by Douglas K. Stuart, *Exodus: A Mentor Commentary* by John L. Mackay, *Exodus: Saved for God's Glory* by Philip Graham Ryken, and *The Message of Exodus: The Days of Our Pilgrimage* by J. A. Motyer.

2. For the purposes of this study, **get a Bible without study notes.** Come on, it's just too easy to look at them. You know I'm right.

3. Though commentaries are initially off-limits, here are some **tools you should use:**

- **Cross-references.** These are the Scripture references in the margin or at the bottom of the page in your Bible. They point you to other passages that deal with the same topic or theme.

- **An English dictionary** to look up unfamiliar words. A good online dictionary is: merriam-webster.com.

- **Other translations of the Bible.** We will use the English Standard Version (ESV) as a starting point, but you can easily consult other versions online. I recommend the Christian Standard Bible (CSB), New International Version (NIV), New American Standard Version (NASB), and the New King James Version (NKJV). Reading more than one translation can expand your understanding of the meaning of a passage. Note: a paraphrase, such as The Message, can be useful but should be regarded as a commentary rather than a translation. They are best consulted after careful study of an actual translation.

- **A printed copy of the text, double-spaced, so you can mark repeated words, phrases, or ideas. For certain lessons in this workbook, portions of the text will be provided for you to mark. If you find it helpful to mark other sections of the text, you should print them and do so.**

STORING UP TREASURE

Approaching God's Word with a God-centered perspective, with context, and with care takes effort and commitment. It is study for the long-term. Some days your study may not move you emotionally or speak to an immediate need. You may not be able to apply a passage at all. But what if ten years from now, in a dark night of the soul, that passage suddenly opens up to you because of the work you have done today? Wouldn't your long-term investment be worth it?

In Matthew 13 we see Jesus begin to teach in parables. He told seven deceptively simple stories that left His disciples struggling for understanding—dwelling in the "I don't know," if you will. After the last parable, He turned to them and asked, "Have you understood all these things?" (v. 51a). Despite their apparent confusion, they answered out of their earnest desire with, "Yes" (v. 51b). Jesus told them that their newfound understanding made them "like the owner of a house who brings out of his storeroom new treasures as well as old" (13:52, NIV).

A storeroom, as Jesus indicated, is a place for keeping valuables over a long period of time for use when needed. Faithful study of God's Word is a means for filling our spiritual storerooms with truth, so that in our hour of need we can bring forth both the old and the new as a source of rich provision. I pray that this study would be for you a source of much treasure and that you would labor well to obtain it.

Grace and peace,

Jen Wilkin

Jen Wilkin

HOW TO USE THIS STUDY

This workbook is designed to be used in a specific way. The homework in the workbook will start you in the process of comprehension, interpretation, and application. However, it was designed to dovetail with small-group discussion time and the teaching sessions. You can use the workbook by itself, but you are likely to find yourself with some unresolved questions. The teaching sessions are intended to resolve most, if not all, of your unanswered questions from the homework and discussion time. **For detailed information about how to access the teaching sessions that accompany this workbook, see page 176.** With this in mind, consider using the materials as follows:

- If you are going through the study **on your own**, first work through the homework, and then watch or listen to the corresponding teaching for that week.

- If you are going through the study **in a group**, first do your homework, and then discuss the questions your group decides to cover. Then watch or listen to the teaching. Some groups watch or listen to the teaching before they meet, which can also work if that format fits best for everyone.

Note: For Week One, there is no homework. The study begins with an audio or video introduction. You will find a Viewer Guide on pages 14–15 that you can use as you watch or listen to the introductory material.

HOW TO USE THE LEADER GUIDE

At the end of each week's homework you will find a leader guide intended to help facilitate discussion in small groups. The leader guide includes questions to help group members compare what they have learned from their homework on Days Two through Five. These questions are either pulled directly from the homework, or they summarize a concept or theme that the homework covered. Each section covers content from a particular day of the homework, first asking group members to observe and then asking them to apply. The observation questions typically ask group members to report a finding or flesh out an interpretation. The application questions challenge them to move beyond intellectual understanding and to identify ways to live differently in light of what they have learned.

As a small group leader, you will want to review these questions before you meet with your group, thinking through your own answers, marking where they occur in the homework, and noting if there are any additional questions you might want to reference to help the flow of the discussion. These questions are suggestions only, intended to help you cover as much ground as you can in a 45-minute discussion time. They should not be seen as requirements or limitations, but as guidelines to help you prepare your group for the teaching time by allowing them to process collectively what they have learned during their homework.

As a facilitator of discussion rather than a teacher, you are allowed and encouraged to be a colearner with your group members. This means you yourself may not always feel confident of your answer to a given question, and that is perfectly OK. Because we are studying for the long-term, we are allowed to leave some questions partially answered or unresolved, trusting for clarity at a later time. In most cases, the teaching time should address any lingering questions that are not resolved in the homework or the small-group discussion time.

ACKNOWLEDGEMENT

I am deeply grateful to Jenni Hamm for her editorial help on this study. Her insights, attention to detail, and love for the Lord and His Word have been indispensable to me. "Let her works praise her in the gates" (Prov. 31:31).

NOTES

Introduction | A Going Out

Who wrote the Book of Exodus?

When was it written?

To whom was it written?

In what style was it written?

What is the central theme of the book?

A Deliverer Delivered

Exodus 1:1–2:10

Having faithfully recorded the history of Israel from Eden to the death of Joseph in the Book of Genesis, Moses continues the story of the people of God in the Book of Exodus. In Genesis Moses told the story of others, but in Exodus he will tell a story in which he himself is a central figure.

READ EXODUS 1:1–2:10.

1. Summarize chapter 1 in two to three sentences.

2. Summarize chapter 2:1-10 in two to three sentences.

3. How would you describe the mood of the story at this point?

NOW LOOK BACK AT EXODUS 1:1-7.

4. As we reviewed in our introductory lesson, Exodus picks up the thread of the redemptive story several hundred years after the death of Joseph. What purpose do verses 1-7 serve in the narrative? Skim through Genesis 46:8-27 to help with your answer.

5. How many of Jacob's descendents are recorded as having gone into Egypt to escape the famine (Ex. 1:5)?

    What does verse 7 tell us happened in the intervening centuries?

    "But the people of Israel were _____ and _____ greatly; they _____ and grew exceedingly strong, so that the land was _____ with them" (ESV).

6. Skim through chapter 1 and note how many times this idea is mentioned. In what other verses does it occur?

7. Moses has deliberately chosen the language of verse 7 and the other verses you noted to make a point. In the chart below, look up each verse and fill in the requested information:

VERSE	TO WHOM WAS GOD SPEAKING?	PROMISE OR COMMAND
Genesis 1:28		
Genesis 9:1		
Genesis 17:2,6		
Genesis 22:17		
Genesis 26:4		
Genesis 28:14		
Genesis 35:11		
Genesis 48:4		

How do these promises in Genesis relate to Exodus 1:7? What does Moses want us to understand?

8. APPLY: Just as Moses reminds his readers of the faithfulness of God with His promises, so we need to be reminded. How have you witnessed God's unfaltering faithfulness to bring about fruitfulness in your life?

DAY THREE

NOW LOOK AT EXODUS 1:8-14.

9. At this point in the story, Joseph is long dead. What does the text mean when it says, ". . . there arose a new king . . . *who did not know* Joseph" (v. 8, *italics mine)*?

10. Specifically, what did this new king fear about the Israelites (vv. 9-10)?

11. What does it mean to "deal shrewdly with" someone (v. 10)? What is the difference between a shrewd person and a smart or wise person? Look up the word *shrewd* in a dictionary and/or thesaurus to help you with your answer.

12. In verse 11, who did the following?

    • Set taskmasters over the Israelites: _____

    • Built the store cities of Pithom and Raamses: _____

13. What word is repeated to emphasize the nature of the treatment the Israelites received (vv. 13-14)?

    Look this word up in a dictionary/thesaurus and list some appropriate synonyms for it:

14. What is the result of the ruthless treatment the Israelites received at the hands of the Egyptians (v. 12)?

15. APPLY: What does this teach us about the God the Israelites served? How is this lesson a comfort to you?

NOW LOOK AT EXODUS 1:15-22.

16. Seeing that his ruthless treatment of the Israelites has failed to subdue them, what does Pharaoh choose for his next strategy (vv. 15-16)?

17. Who thwarts the plans of Pharaoh (vv. 17-19)?

18. The Egyptians worshiped their pharaohs as gods. What do you think would have happened to Shiphrah and Puah if Pharaoh had uncovered their deception?

19. What is God's response to the actions of Shiphrah and Puah (vv. 20-21)?

20. APPLY: What is *your* response to the actions of Shiphrah and Puah? How are they worthy of your admiration and imitation? List some thoughts below:

21. Commentaries frequently emphasize that the midwives lied to Pharaoh when he asked why they had not obeyed his murderous command. We will discuss it further in the teaching time, but for now, what is your response to this line of thought? If the midwives were lying, were they wrong to do so?

22. Seeing that his ruthless plan to have the midwives murder all the male Israelite babies has failed, what does Pharaoh choose for his next strategy (v. 22)?

23. APPLY: Think of a time when you were pressured to do wrong in order to preserve a job or relationship. How did you handle that situation? How should having a fear of the Lord shape our responses to times like those?

NOW LOOK AT EXODUS 2:1-10.

24. In the space below is a list of each of the people mentioned in these ten verses. Skim through the passage. Next to the character, write his or her proper name if you find it in the text.

Verse 1   a man from the house of Levi   _____

Verse 1   his wife, a Levite woman   _____

Verse 2   a fine child, hidden for three months   _____

Verse 4   the child's sister   _____

Verse 5   the daughter of Pharaoh   _____

Did you only find one proper name? What explanation would you give for how this passage is written? Why is only one name given?

25. Now let's try to fill in a few more blanks. Look up the following verses and fill in the names they contain next to their owners in the blanks above:

Exodus 6:20 | Exodus 15:20 | Numbers 26:59

(Remember that, as we learned in the teaching time last week, Pharaoh was never named. It follows that we would not know his daughter's name either.)

26. What was the baby doing that caused Pharaoh's daughter to take pity on him in the basket (v. 6)?

27. What sweet arrangement does God devise through Miriam's words and actions (vv. 7-9)?

28. Why do you think Jochebed places her baby in a basket among the reeds? What outcome do you think she expects, hopes for, or fears?

29. Genesis tells a similar story of a mother in a desperate situation. Having been cast out by her mistress, Sarah, Hagar wanders with her young son into the desert to face certain death. She places the child under a tree where he lies crying in his misery. Read Genesis 21:15-16 to find out why she does this. How might Hagar's story shed light on Jochebed's actions?

NOW LOOK AT GENESIS 21:17-20a FOR THE REST OF HAGAR'S STORY:

[17] And God heard the voice of the boy, and the angel of God called to Hagar from heaven and said to her, "What troubles you, Hagar? Fear not, for God has heard the voice of the boy where he is. [18] Up! Lift up the boy, and hold him fast with your hand, for I will make him into a great nation." [19] Then God opened her eyes, and she saw a well of water. And she went and filled the skin with water and gave the boy a drink. [20] And God was with the boy, and he grew up.

How tender the tracings of the hand of God on the lives of these two women and their similar stories: a child's cry heard by One who can save, a son with a destiny to fulfill, and a mother who holds the drink necessary for him to live.

30. APPLY: How should these two stories of Hagar and Jochebed instruct us when we find ourselves in a seemingly hopeless situation? What do these stories teach us about the character of God?

31. When he is brought to her, Pharaoh's daughter names the baby Moses. What does the name mean? (See Ex. 2:10.) How is it appropriate?

32. APPLY: Moses is taken into the care of the very household that had decreed his death. Think of a time God granted you favor with an enemy. What did that situation teach you about His faithfulness? His power over human hearts?

WRAP-UP

Did you see evidence of the theme of deliverance in this week's passage? If so, where?

What aspect of God's character has this week's passage of Exodus shown you more clearly? *(Note: Each week we will end our homework by focusing on what the text has revealed about God. A list of God's attributes can be found in the back of your workbook on pages 172–173 to help you think through your answer to the wrap-up questions.)*

Fill in the following statement:

Knowing that God is ⬚⬚⬚⬚⬚⬚⬚⬚⬚⬚ **shows me that I am** ⬚⬚⬚⬚⬚⬚⬚⬚ .

What one step can you take this week to better live in light of this truth?

NOTES

1. OBSERVE: (question 4, p. 19) As we reviewed in our introductory lesson, Exodus picks up the thread of the redemptive story several hundred years after the death of Joseph. What purpose does Exodus 1:1-7 serve in the narrative? Skim through Genesis 46:8-27 to help with your answer.

APPLY: (question 8, p. 20) Just as Moses reminds his readers of the faithfulness of God with His promises, so we need to be reminded. How have you witnessed God's unfaltering faithfulness to bring about fruitfulness in your life?

2. OBSERVE: (question 14, p. 22) What is the result of the ruthless treatment the Israelites received at the hands of the Egyptians (Ex. 1:12)?

APPLY: (question 15, p. 22) What does this teach us about the God the Israelites served? How is this lesson a comfort to you?

3. OBSERVE: (question 18, p. 23) The Egyptians worshiped their pharaohs as gods. What do you think would have happened to Shiphrah and Puah if Pharaoh had uncovered their deception?

APPLY: (question 20, p. 23) What is *your* response to the actions of Shiphrah and Puah? How are they worthy of your admiration and imitation?

4. OBSERVE: (question 21, p. 23) Commentaries frequently emphasize that the midwives lied to Pharaoh when he asked why they had not obeyed his murderous command. We will discuss it further in the teaching time, but for now, what is your response to this line of thought? If the midwives were lying, were they wrong to do so?

APPLY: (question 23, p. 24) Think of a time when you were pressured to do wrong in order to preserve a job or relationship. How did you handle that situation? How should having a fear of the Lord shape our responses to times like those?

APPLY: (question 30, p. 27) How should these two stories of Hagar and Jochebed instruct us when we find ourselves in a seemingly hopeless situation? What do these stories teach us about the character of God?

5. **OBSERVE:** (question 31, p. 27) When he is brought to her, Pharaoh's daughter names the baby Moses. What does the name mean? (See Ex. 2:10.) How is it appropriate?

APPLY: (question 32, p. 27) Moses is taken into the care of the very household that had decreed his death. Think of a time God granted you favor with an enemy. What did that situation teach you about His faithfulness? His power over human hearts?

6. **WRAP-UP:** (p. 28) What aspect of God's character has this week's passage of Exodus shown you more clearly?

Fill in the following statement:

Knowing that God is ⎯⎯⎯⎯⎯⎯⎯⎯⎯⎯ **shows me that I am** ⎯⎯⎯⎯⎯⎯⎯⎯⎯⎯ **.**

What one step can you take this week to better live in light of this truth?

WEEK TWO | VIEWER GUIDE NOTES

A Leader Prepared

Exodus 2:11–3:22

Moses, the future deliverer of Israel, finds deliverance in his infancy through the intervention of five women. Having been saved from death, he must now be equipped for the work of ministry that lies ahead. Our passage this week traces his course from prince to fugitive to prophet.

READ EXODUS 2:11–3:22.

1. Summarize chapter 2:11-25 in two to three sentences.

2. Summarize chapter 3 in two to three sentences.

3. In Acts chapter 7 Stephen preaches a sermon in which he recounts the history of Israel. Look up Acts 7:20-34 and note how Stephen summarizes this week's section of Exodus. What additional insights do we gain from his account? Keep a bookmark there. We'll reference this passage again during our study.

NOW LOOK AT EXODUS 2:11-15.

At the end of last week's lesson, we saw Moses go to be raised in the house of Pharaoh as a son of the princess (Ex. 2:10). We do not know how long he stayed with his parents Amram and Jochebed. He may have stayed only until he was weaned (age two or three), or he may have stayed until he was past early childhood.

4. How might Moses' actions toward the Egyptian in verses 11-12 argue that he spent a longer childhood in the home of his Hebrew birth parents?

5. What does Acts 7:25 indicate was Moses' motive for killing the Egyptian? Does this motive justify his actions?

6. Why does Moses flee to Midian (Ex. 2:15)?

7. APPLY: Moses' response to injustice was fueled by unchecked emotion, deteriorated into violence, and resulted in failure. What methods of dealing with injustice are more likely to prosper? List some thoughts below.

What injustice do you want to confront? How can you more faithfully employ some of the methods you listed above?

NOW LOOK AT EXODUS 2:16-22.

8. Write down the names and details of Moses' new family members:

    Father-in-law

    Wife

    How many sisters-in-law?

    Firstborn son

9. What is the meaning of the name Moses chooses for his son (v. 22)?

    How is this name a fitting one for a Hebrew baby in Moses' time? Look up Hebrews 11:8-10,13-14 to see who else was described in similar terms. Note their names below.

NOW LOOK AT EXODUS 2:23-25.

10. What does verse 23 indicate about how long Moses was in Midian?

11. What did the Israelites do during this time? Write the two verb phrases you find that describe their actions in verse 23.

   1.

   2.

12. What did God do during this time? Note the four verb phrases that describe His actions in verses 24-25.

   1.

   2.

   3.

   4.

13. Look up the word *covenant* in a dictionary or thesaurus and write a synonym for it that best fits the way it is used in verse 24.

14. What was the covenant that God made with Abraham, Isaac, and Jacob? Look at Genesis 17:1-6 to refresh your memory.

15. What is the tone of the end of Exodus 2? Check the answer you think best applies:

____ forlorn

____ expectant

____ ominous

____ joyful

16. APPLY: How would the words in verses 24-25 have been a comfort to Moses' original readers, Israelites about to enter the promised land? How should they comfort us?

NOW LOOK AT EXODUS 3:1-6.

17. What mountain does Moses lead his flock to?

"... _____, the mountain of God" (v. 1).

What other name do you learn for this mountain in Acts 7:30?

Mount _____

18. What occupation is Moses pursuing at the beginning of this passage (v. 1)?

He was a _____.

Can you think of other well-known people in the Bible who also held this occupation? List their names below:

19. How might the experience of herding animals serve to prepare Moses for his future?

20. What strange sight catches Moses' attention (vv. 2-3)?

21. Why do you think God chooses to appear to Moses in this particular form?

Why does God warn Moses to keep his distance and remove his sandals (v. 5)?

22. As we move through the Book of Exodus, we'll see Moses met with God multiple times. How does Moses feel about his first close encounter with the presence of God (v. 6)?

Is Moses wrong to feel this way? Why or why not?

23. Why do you think God identifies Himself the way He does in verse 6? What does He want Moses to understand?

24. APPLY: Have you ever experienced an overwhelming sense of the holiness of God? Can you identify with Moses' instinctive covering of his face? What impact should a revelation of the holiness of God have on us?

NOW LOOK AT EXODUS 3:7-12.

25. In the blanks below, summarize each statement God made about Himself:

Verse 7   "I _____."

Verse 7   "[I] _____."

Verse 7   "I _____."

Verse 8   "I _____."

Verse 9   "I _____."

Verse 10   "I _____."

Based on what you wrote above, who has a handle on the situation in Egypt?

26. After hearing God's plan, what objection does Moses raise in verse 11? Rewrite this verse in your own words to capture Moses' meaning.

27. How does God answer Moses' objection (v. 12)? Do you think this is the answer Moses expected? Why or why not?

NOW LOOK AT VERSES 13-22.

28. Having heard God's reiteration of His intention to send him to deliver Israel out of Egypt, does Moses respond with confidence and willing submission (v. 13)?

___ Yes ___ No

What is Moses' next point of concern with God's plan?

29. How does God respond to his concern (vv. 14-15)?

30. Of all the names God could have given for Himself, why do you think He chooses "I AM WHO I AM" (v. 14) for Moses to take back to the people of Israel? What do you think this name is intended to reveal about the character of God?

31. In addition to giving His name, what specific instructions does God give to Moses (vv. 16-17)? Summarize them below.

What does God say will happen if Moses does as He has said (v. 18a)?

32. What does God say the elders and Moses should say to Pharaoh (v. 18b)?

Will Pharaoh agree to this plan (v. 19)?

___ Yes ___ No

What does God indicate He will do to change Pharaoh's mind (v. 20)?

33. Whose hand is the subject of verses 19-20?

What will that hand accomplish? Check the best answer:

___ Israelites will be set free, barely escaping with their lives.
___ Israelites will be set free, walking out unharmed but empty-handed.
___ Israelites will be set free, carrying the wealth of the Egyptians with them.

34. APPLY: Have you ever thought or said, *If God would just tell me plainly what to do, I would do it*? How does the story of Moses and the burning bush challenge that statement? Why do we still hesitate to obey even when the will of God is plain?

WRAP-UP

Did you see evidence of the theme of deliverance in this week's passage? If so, where?

What aspect of God's character has this week's passage of Exodus shown you more clearly?

Fill in the following statement:

Knowing that God is _____ **shows me that I am** _____ .

What one step can you take this week to better live in light of this truth?

NOTES

1. **OBSERVE:** (question 5, p. 37) What does Acts 7:25 indicate was Moses' motive for killing the Egyptian? Does this motive justify his actions?

   APPLY: (question 7, p. 37) Moses' response to injustice was fueled by unchecked emotion, deteriorated into violence, and resulted in failure. What methods of dealing with injustice are more likely to prosper? What injustice do you want to confront? How can you more faithfully employ some of the methods you listed?

2. **OBSERVE:** (question 14, p. 39) What was the covenant that God made with Abraham, Isaac, and Jacob? Look at Genesis 17:1-6 to refresh your memory.

   APPLY: (question 16, p. 40) How would the words of Exodus 2:24-25 have been a comfort to Moses' original readers, Israelites about to enter the promised land? How should they comfort us?

3. **OBSERVE:** (question 23, p. 42) Why do you think God identifies Himself the way He does in Exodus 3:6? What does He want Moses to understand?

   APPLY: (question 24, p. 42) Have you ever experienced an overwhelming sense of the holiness of God? Can you identify with Moses' instinctive covering of his face? What impact should a revelation of the holiness of God have on us?

4. **OBSERVE:** (question 31, p. 44) In addition to giving His name, what specific instructions does God give to Moses (Ex. 3:16-17)? What does God say will happen if Moses does as He has said (v. 18a)?

   APPLY: (question 34, p. 45) Have you ever thought or said, *If God would just tell me plainly what to do, I would do it*? How does the story of Moses and the burning bush challenge that statement? Why do we still hesitate to obey even when the will of God is plain?

5. **WRAP-UP:** (p. 46) What aspect of God's character has this week's passage of Exodus shown you more clearly?

Fill in the following statement:

Knowing that God is _____ **shows me that
I am** _____ .

What one step can you take this week to better live in light of this truth?

Sent Back to Egypt

Exodus 4

Far from his home, shepherding a flock at the foot of a mountain, Moses learns that his destiny is to shepherd another flock to the foot of Mount Horeb. God has indeed set him apart to deliver his people from Egypt. But despite the Lord's assurances, Moses' doubts persist.

READ EXODUS 4.

1. At the end of last week's lesson, we heard Moses consider God's command to serve as Israel's deliverer. He raised two objections. What were they?

   Exodus 3:11

   Exodus 3:13

2. Summarize Exodus 4:1-17 in two to three sentences.

3. Summarize Exodus 4:18-31 in two to three sentences.

NOW LOOK AT EXODUS 4:1-9.

4. After being told three times of God's certain plan to free the Israelites with Moses as His chosen deliverer, is Moses sold on the plan (v. 1)?

___ Yes ___ No

What is his concern? (Be specific—whom does he fear will not believe him?)

5. What is God's solution to Moses' third objection?

6. Look back at your answer to question 33 from last week (p. 45). Now notice the contrast in verses 2-7. Whose hand is the subject?

What will that hand accomplish? Check the best answer:

___ Miraculous signs to convince the people
___ Miraculous signs to convince Pharaoh
___ Absolutely nothing, of its own power

7. APPLY: Have you ever offered up repeated objections to God's plan? How did God respond to your objections? What did His response reveal about His character?

NOW LOOK AT EXODUS 4:10-17.

8. With the promise of two really great signs and a third for backup, is Moses done raising objections to God's sovereign plans?

___ Yes ___ No

9. What is Moses' fourth objection to the plan (v. 10)?

10. How does God respond to his objection? In essence, what does God say (vv. 11-12)?

11. What do the first three words of verse 12 tell you about God's patience with Moses at this point in the conversation?

12. In verse 13 Moses makes a fifth and final objection—the most honest of them all. How would you paraphrase what he says? Rewrite his words in your own.

What is God's response?

*"Then the _____ of the L*ORD *was _____ against Moses" (v. 14a, ESV).*

13. APPLY: Look up James 1:19-20. How was God "slow to anger" in His dealings with Moses? Are you slow to anger? How should the story of the burning bush change the way you handle your anger toward others?

NOW LOOK AT EXODUS 4:18-23.

14. Glance back at Stephen's words in Acts 7:30. If Moses was forty when he came to Midian, how old is he now?

15. Acts 7:22 tells us that while Moses was growing up in Egypt, he was "instructed in all the wisdom of the Egyptians, and he was mighty in his words and deeds." What further necessary "education" do you think he received in Midian? List some thoughts below.

16. What has happened to Moses' shepherding staff? (See Ex. 4:20.) How is this fitting for Moses' new job description as the leader of the people of Israel?

17. The concept of God hardening Pharaoh's heart (v. 21) has been the topic of much discussion by theologians. We will discuss it in our teaching time, but for now, based on your knowledge of where the story of Exodus is heading and based on your understanding of both the justice and mercy of God as revealed in Scripture, what do you think it means that God hardened Pharaoh's heart?

18. APPLY: What fear lay at the root of all of Moses' objections to God? Give an example of how this same fear could prevent you from doing what the Lord has clearly asked you to do. What realization must we (and Moses) reach before we can move forward in confident obedience?

NOW LOOK AT EXODUS 4:24-26.

Okay, so it just got weird. Let's see if we can sort through this. Read Genesis 17:9-14 and answer the following questions:

19. What did God command would be the sign of His covenant with Abraham and his descendants?

20. How many times in Genesis 17:9-14 is the command to be circumcised given?

    Why do you think this is so?

21. Upon whom was the sign to be carried out?

22. At what age was the sign to be carried out?

23. What was the penalty for failure to observe the sign of the covenant (v. 14)?

24. Do you think Moses was circumcised? Why or why not?

25. Based on Zipporah's actions in Exodus 4:25, what had Moses left undone? Do you think this omission was made in ignorance? Why or why not?

26. What important lesson do you think Moses learned about obedience from this incident?

27. APPLY: Moses could not act as God's representative to the people while disregarding God's requirement of circumcision. Can you effectively act as God's representative if you disregard God's commands for holy living? Think of an example to illustrate your answer.

NOW LOOK AT EXODUS 4:27-31.

28. What important person are we introduced to in verse 27?

29. Based on what you know of Moses' early years, how well do you think he and his brother know each other at this point?

30. How many times does the text record that Aaron objected to God's command to go in search of his brother? What does this reveal about Aaron's character?

31. Do verses 28-30 relate a story of obedience or disobedience to the will of God?

32. What remarkable phrase begins verse 31?

    What remarkable phrase ends verse 31?

33. APPLY: What does Moses' story thus far teach us about man's ability to thwart God's plans or refuse His commands? How does this comfort you? How does it warn you?

Did you see evidence of the theme of deliverance in this week's passage?
If so, where?

What aspect of God's character has this week's passage of Exodus shown you
more clearly?

Fill in the following statement:

Knowing that God is _____ **shows me that**
I am _____ .

What one step can you take this week to better live in light of this truth?

1. OBSERVE: (question 5, p. 55) What is God's solution to Moses' third objection?

APPLY: (question 7, p. 55) Have you ever offered up repeated objections to God's plan? How did God respond to your objections? What did His response reveal about His character?

2. OBSERVE: (question 11, p. 56) What do the first three words of Exodus 4:12 tell you about God's patience with Moses at this point in the conversation?

APPLY: (question 13, p. 56) Look up James 1:19-20. How was God "slow to anger" in His dealings with Moses? Are you slow to anger? How should the story of the burning bush change the way you handle your anger toward others?

3. OBSERVE: (question 16, p. 57) What has happened to Moses' shepherding staff? (See Ex. 4:20.) How is this fitting for Moses' new job description as the leader of the people of Israel?

APPLY: (question 18, p. 57) What fear lay at the root of all of Moses' objections to God? Give an example of how this same fear could prevent you from doing what the Lord has clearly asked you to do. What realization must we (and Moses) reach before we can move forward in confident obedience?

4. OBSERVE: (question 25, p. 59) Based on Zipporah's actions in Exodus 4:25, what had Moses left undone? Do you think this omission was made in ignorance? Why or why not?

APPLY: (question 27, p. 59) Moses could not act as God's representative to the people while disregarding God's requirement of circumcision. Can you effectively act as God's representative if you disregard God's commands for holy living? Think of an example to illustrate your answer.

5. **OBSERVE:** (question 31, p. 60) Does Exodus 4:28-30 relate a story of obedience or disobedience to the will of God?

APPLY: (question 33, p. 60) What does Moses' story thus far teach us about man's ability to thwart God's plans or refuse His commands? How does this comfort you? How does it warn you?

6. **WRAP-UP:** (p. 61) What aspect of God's character has this week's passage of Exodus shown you more clearly?

Fill in the following statement:

Knowing that God is _____ **shows me that I am** _____ .

What one step can you take this week to better live in light of this truth?

WEEK FOUR | VIEWER GUIDE NOTES

Opposition and Unbelief

Exodus 5:1–6:27

With his objections silenced, his family brought into "covenantal compliance," and his brother at his side, Moses returns to Egypt to tell his people of God's plan for their deliverance. His words are met with belief and worshipful reverence to God. His confidence in the message entrusted to him must have been high as he moved toward his next act of obedience: an audience with Pharaoh. But no simple conversation awaits him.

READ EXODUS 5:1–6:27.

1. Summarize chapter 5 in two to three sentences.

2. Summarize chapter 6:1-27 in two to three sentences.

3. The theme of opposition runs throughout chapters 5–6. We will examine it as we move through this week's lesson. Glance back through the text and, in the space below, briefly note who opposes whom and why:

NOW LOOK BACK AT EXODUS 5:1-14.

4. What request do Aaron and Moses make of Pharaoh (v. 1)?

5. What is Pharaoh's response (v. 2)? Paraphrase his answer in your own words.

6. How do Moses and Aaron change their request when they made it a second time (v. 3)? What additions do they make? Why do you think this is so?

7. What is Pharaoh's second response to their request (vv. 4-5)? Paraphrase his answer in your own words.

8. What steps does Pharaoh take to keep the Israelites subdued (vv. 6-9)? What do you think is his motive for devising this plan?

9. Using context clues, what is the nationality of the foremen (vv. 10-14)? Why would Pharaoh place Israelites in a position of authority?

10. What advantage do you think Pharaoh hopes to gain by scattering the Israelites throughout the land to gather stubble? Why not just continue giving them the straw and raise their quota of bricks (v. 12)?

11. Who are the first to be punished when the quotas are not met (v. 14)? How is this a good strategy on Pharaoh's part?

12. APPLY: When you encounter difficulty while pursuing God's will, how do you respond? Is it right to expect the path of God's will to be free from conflict? Why or why not?

NOW LOOK AT EXODUS 5:15-23.

13. To whom do the foremen take their complaint (vv. 15-16)? Does this surprise you? What does it tell you about their standing with Pharaoh?

14. What is Pharaoh's response (vv. 17-18)? Paraphrase his answer in your own words.

15. Do the foremen react with anger toward Pharaoh (vv. 19-21)? Where do they lay the blame for their difficulties?

16. What is Moses' response to the accusation of the foremen (vv. 22-23)? Does he direct his frustration at them?

What emotions do you hear in his response?

Does his response surprise you? Why or why not?

NOW LOOK AT EXODUS 6:1-9.

17. How might God have justly responded to the angry despair of Moses?

18. What does God's response reveal about His character yet again? Look up the following verses to help you with your answer. Note the repeated theme:

    Numbers 14:18 | Psalm 86:15 | Psalm 103:8 | Psalm 145:8

19. How might Moses benefit from learning to be slow to anger? Look up the following verses and note the benefit each verse mentions:

    Proverbs 14:29 | Proverbs 16:32 | Proverbs 19:11

20. APPLY: What situation or person causes you to be quick to anger? What spiritual truth from the two previous questions do you most need to meditate on?

21. As He did at the burning bush, God articulates His plan for deliverance as a sovereign act He will accomplish. In the space below, list every statement in Exodus 6:2-8 that begins with the word *I*.

What is the clear point of verses 2-8?

22. How do the people respond to the message when Moses delivers it (v. 9)?
Look back at Exodus 4:30-31 and note the change in their response.
According to Exodus 6:9, what accounts for the difference?

23. APPLY: It has often been noted with a wink that ministry would be easy if it
weren't for all the people you have to deal with. Have you found this to be
true? Why are those who need ministry often so hard to help? How can we
avoid discouragement and frustration as we faithfully minister?

NOW LOOK AT EXODUS 6:10-13.

24. Immediately on the heels of his failed speech to his own people, to whom is
Moses sent to speak next?

25. We will discuss this in the teaching time, but what do you think Moses
means by the phrase "I am of uncircumcised lips" (v. 12)? Give your best
explanation below. Look up Isaiah 6:5 to see a similar statement made by
the prophet Isaiah when confronted by the holiness of God.

26. What idea does verse 13 reinforce? Is God's plan merely a suggestion to Moses and Aaron?

27. APPLY: What clear command of God are you most likely to question or downgrade to a suggestion? Why is this a dangerous practice?

DAY FIVE

NOW LOOK AT EXODUS 6:14-27. NO, REALLY. READ IT.

Hooray for genealogies! All Scripture is profitable for our instruction, and this passage is no exception. Some of the names listed here will figure prominently in later Old Testament passages. Let's spend some time here so that we will recognize who they are when the time comes.

28. The purpose of the genealogy is disclosed to us in verses 26-27. Whose identity and heritage are we meant to understand?

_____ and _____

29. In the space below, fill in the family tree we find in verses 14-27. With a highlighter, trace the path from Moses and Aaron back to Israel.

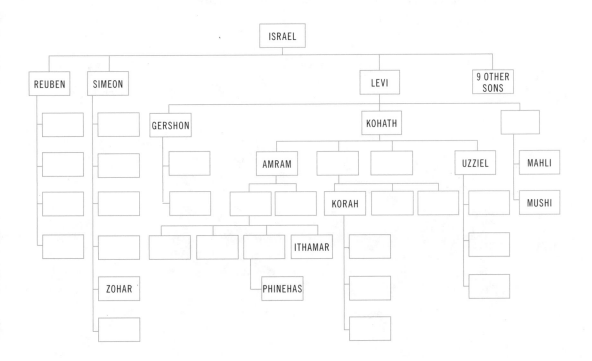

30. Why do you think we are reminded of the lineage of Moses and Aaron at this point in the story? What purpose does this genealogy serve? We'll discuss it in the teaching time, but give your best guess.

31. APPLY: Just like Moses and Aaron, you have been given a work to do that only you can do. The full extent of that work may not yet be clear to you, but what parts of it are? In the space below, note what work you know the Lord has given you to do. Then pause to pray. Ask Him to embolden you to do your work regardless of opposition and difficulty.

WRAP-UP

Did you see evidence of the theme of deliverance in this week's passage? If so, where?

What aspect of God's character has this week's passage of Exodus shown you more clearly?

Fill in the following statement:

Knowing that God is   **shows me that I am**   **.**

What one step can you take this week to better live in light of this truth?

1. OBSERVE: (question 16, p. 71) What is Moses' response to the accusation of the foremen (Ex. 5:22-23)? Does he direct his frustration at them? What emotions do you hear in his response? Does his response surprise you? Why or why not?

APPLY: (question 12, p. 70) When you encounter difficulty while pursuing God's will, how do you respond? Is it right to expect the path of God's will to be free from conflict? Why or why not?

2. OBSERVE: (question 18, p. 72) What does God's response reveal about His character yet again? Look up the following verses to help you with your answer. Note the repeated theme:
Proverbs 14:29 | Proverbs 16:32 | Proverbs 19:11

APPLY: (question 20, p. 72) What situation or person causes you to be quick to anger? What spiritual truth from the two previous questions do you most need to meditate on?

3. OBSERVE: (question 21, pp. 72–73) As He did at the burning bush, God articulates His plan for deliverance as a sovereign act He will accomplish. What is the clear point of Exodus 6:2-8?

APPLY: (question 23, p. 73) It has often been noted with a wink that ministry would be easy if it weren't for all the people you have to deal with. Have you found this to be true? Why are those who need ministry often so hard to help? How can we avoid discouragement and frustration as we faithfully minister?

4. OBSERVE: (question 26, p. 74) What idea does Exodus 6:13 reinforce? Is God's plan merely a suggestion to Moses and Aaron?

APPLY: (question 27, p. 74) What clear command of God are you most likely to question or downgrade to a suggestion? Why is this a dangerous practice?

APPLY: (question 31, p. 76) Just like Moses and Aaron, you have been given a work to do that only you can do. The full extent of that work may not yet be clear to you, but what parts of it are? What work has the Lord given you to do? How emboldened do you feel to step into it? What holds you back?

5. WRAP-UP: (p. 77) What aspect of God's character has this week's passage of Exodus shown you more clearly?

Fill in the following statement:

Knowing that God is _____ **shows me that I am** _____ .

What one step can you take this week to better live in light of this truth?

WEEK FIVE | VIEWER GUIDE NOTES

Plagues

Exodus 6:28–10:29

This week's lesson will flow a little differently than the previous lessons. We will cover four chapters that detail the first nine plagues the Lord sends against Egypt. Next week, we will examine the tenth and final plague.

You will need a yellow highlighter and a set of colored pencils to complete this week's lesson. In order to understand the structure of the plague narrative, we will be marking repeated phrases and ideas in this section of the text. A copy of the text is provided for this purpose at the back of this lesson (pp. 91–99).

Before we get to the plagues, our author gives us a brief introductory section.

READ EXODUS 6:28–7:13.

1. Summarize this section in two to three sentences.

2. What portion of this section retells what we know so far? Why do you think we are given this reminder at this point in the narrative?

3. In 7:8-13, what happened when Moses and Aaron gave the sign that was intended to prove their authority from God?

4. APPLY: Have you ever asked God to give you a physical sign? Why should we trust the promises of God more than physical signs of His presence?

NOW READ EXODUS 7:14–10:29 USING THE COPY PRINTED AT THE END OF THIS LESSON.

The narrative is structured with carefully repeated phrases that occur in a specific order. We will be marking the text to get a visual picture of its structure. For each plague, note the text in the following way:

5. In the left-hand margin next to the beginning of each new plague, write its number and circle it. You should have nine circled numbers.

6. Under each circled number, draw a simple picture to illustrate the plague it indicates.

Now let's look for repeated phrases.

7. At the opening to each plague account, underline in red the phrase "the LORD said to Moses." This phrase occurs in each of the nine accounts.

You may have noticed as you read that the plagues are told in three groups of three: plagues 1–3, 4–6, and 7–9 are written with parallel structure. As you mark the following phrases, notice how each occurs once in its set of three plagues:

8. On plagues 1, 4, and 7 (the first of each set), underline in blue the phrase indicating what time Moses and Aaron were to seek out Pharaoh. *(Hint: it should follow the phrase you just underlined in red.)*

9. On plagues 2, 5, and 8 (the second of each set) underline in purple the phrase "Go in to Pharaoh." *(Hint: it should follow the phrase you just underlined in red.)*

10. On plagues 3, 6, and 9, notice there is no "Go to Pharaoh" phrase following the phrase you underlined in red.

11. **APPLY:** Why do you think the account of the plagues is written in such a repetitive, structured manner? How would this approach have helped Moses' original audience? How does it help us today?

Now, let's continue to mark phrases that occur consistently throughout the nine plagues.

12. Underline in turquoise the phrase "And the LORD said to Moses, 'Say to Aaron, "Take your staff and stretch out your hand . . ."'" It will be worded slightly different in each account. In some, it is implied.

13. Highlight in yellow the phrases indicating that Moses and/or Aaron did as the Lord commanded, or that the Lord did as He had said He would do.

14. Draw an orange box around the phrase "Then Pharaoh called Moses and Aaron." It will be worded slightly different in each account. Draw an orange bracket in the margin to note sections of negotiation between Pharaoh and Moses.

    During which five plagues do they occur?

    Generally, what is the pattern for how these negotiations go?

    • What does Pharaoh ask and promise?

    • How does Moses respond?

    • What does Pharaoh do when the plague is removed?

    • As the plagues progressed, how do Pharaoh's compromises change?

15. APPLY: When seeking to obey God, do we ever look for a compromise that covers most of what He requires instead of obeying completely? Give an example.

16. In the text, underline in <u>green</u> every phrase that mentions the hardness of Pharaoh's heart. Of the nine plague descriptions, how many contain a statement about this?

17. Now let's summarize a little of what we have seen through marking the text. Fill in the chart below with your observations:

PLAGUE	DESCRIPTION	DOES WHAT GOD HAS SAID COME TO PASS?	DOES PHARAOH NEGOTIATE?	OUTCOME
1	Water to blood	Yes	No	Heart hardened; Israel in bondage
2				
3				
4				
5				
6				
7				
8				
9				

18. <u>APPLY:</u> Have you ever made promises to God when you were in a crisis and then set them aside once the crisis had passed? Why do we tend to do this? What does this kind of behavior indicate we believe is true about God? About us?

19. List the character trait(s) consistently displayed by each major figure in this section of the narrative. What adjectives best describe each of them?

GOD	MOSES	AARON

20. Do you see any significance to the order of the plagues? Why do you think God orders them as He does? Give some thoughts below:

21. Do you see any significance to the nature of the plagues? Why do you think God chooses the types of disasters He does? Give some thoughts below:

22. Note the story line of the magicians of Egypt. They are mentioned in plagues 1, 2, 3, and 6.

- How many plagues are they able to counterfeit with their "secret arts"?

- What correct conclusion do the magicians reach in plague 3 (8:19)?

- What do you think the author wants us to understand based on the magicians' reaction to plague number 6 (9:11)?

23. APPLY: Pharaoh was unwilling to give up his perceived right to keep the Israelites as his slaves. Even in the face of great opposition, he clung to his own will rather than submitting to the will of God. Is there a disobedient area of your heart that is hardened to the truth? What steps can you take to submit it to the softening power of the Holy Spirit?

WRAP-UP

Did you see evidence of the theme of deliverance in this week's passage? If so, where?

What aspect of God's character has this week's passage of Exodus shown you more clearly?

Fill in the following statement:

Knowing that God is   **shows me that I am**   .

What one step can you take this week to better live in light of this truth?

Exodus 7:14–10:29
THE FIRST PLAGUE: WATER TURNED TO BLOOD

7 ¹⁴ Then the LORD said to Moses, "Pharaoh's heart is hardened; he refuses to let the people

go. ¹⁵ Go to Pharaoh in the morning, as he is going out to the water. Stand on the bank of

the Nile to meet him, and take in your hand the staff that turned into a serpent.

¹⁶ And you shall say to him, 'The LORD, the God of the Hebrews, sent me to you, saying,

"Let my people go, that they may serve me in the wilderness." But so far, you have not

obeyed. ¹⁷ Thus says the LORD, "By this you shall know that I am the LORD: behold, with

the staff that is in my hand I will strike the water that is in the Nile, and it shall turn into

blood. ¹⁸ The fish in the Nile shall die, and the Nile will stink, and the Egyptians will grow

weary of drinking water from the Nile."'" ¹⁹ And the LORD said to Moses, "Say to Aaron,

'Take your staff and stretch out your hand over the waters of Egypt, over their rivers, their

canals, and their ponds, and all their pools of water, so that they may become blood, and

there shall be blood throughout all the land of Egypt, even in vessels of wood and in

vessels of stone.'"

²⁰ Moses and Aaron did as the LORD commanded. In the sight of Pharaoh and in the sight of

his servants he lifted up the staff and struck the water in the Nile, and all the water in the Nile

turned into blood. ²¹ And the fish in the Nile died, and the Nile stank, so that the Egyptians

could not drink water from the Nile. There was blood throughout all the land of Egypt. ²² But

the magicians of Egypt did the same by their secret arts. So Pharaoh's heart remained hardened,

and he would not listen to them, as the LORD had said. ²³ Pharaoh turned and went into his

house, and he did not take even this to heart. ²⁴ And all the Egyptians dug along the Nile for

water to drink, for they could not drink the water of the Nile.

[25] Seven full days passed after the Lord had struck the Nile.

THE SECOND PLAGUE: FROGS

8 Then the Lord said to Moses, "Go in to Pharaoh and say to him, 'Thus says the Lord, "Let my people go, that they may serve me. [2] But if you refuse to let them go, behold, I will plague all your country with frogs. [3] The Nile shall swarm with frogs that shall come up into your house and into your bedroom and on your bed and into the houses of your servants and your people, and into your ovens and your kneading bowls. [4] The frogs shall come up on you and on your people and on all your servants."'" [5] And the Lord said to Moses, "Say to Aaron, 'Stretch out your hand with your staff over the rivers, over the canals and over the pools, and make frogs come up on the land of Egypt!'" [6] So Aaron stretched out his hand over the waters of Egypt, and the frogs came up and covered the land of Egypt. [7] But the magicians did the same by their secret arts and made frogs come up on the land of Egypt.

[8] Then Pharaoh called Moses and Aaron and said, "Plead with the Lord to take away the frogs from me and from my people, and I will let the people go to sacrifice to the Lord." [9] Moses said to Pharaoh, "Be pleased to command me when I am to plead for you and for your servants and for your people, that the frogs be cut off from you and your houses and be left only in the Nile." [10] And he said, "Tomorrow." Moses said, "Be it as you say, so that you may know that there is no one like the Lord our God. [11] The frogs shall go away from you and your houses and your servants and your people. They shall be left only in the Nile." [12] So Moses and Aaron went out from Pharaoh, and Moses cried to the Lord about the frogs, as he had agreed with Pharaoh. [13] And the Lord did according to the word of Moses. The frogs died out in the houses, the courtyards, and the fields. [14] And they gathered them

together in heaps, and the land stank. [15] But when Pharaoh saw that there was a respite, he hardened his heart and would not listen to them, as the Lord had said.

THE THIRD PLAGUE: GNATS

[16] Then the Lord said to Moses, "Say to Aaron, 'Stretch out your staff and strike the dust of the earth, so that it may become gnats in all the land of Egypt.'" [17] And they did so. Aaron stretched out his hand with his staff and struck the dust of the earth, and there were gnats on man and beast. All the dust of the earth became gnats in all the land of Egypt. [18] The magicians tried by their secret arts to produce gnats, but they could not. So there were gnats on man and beast. [19] Then the magicians said to Pharaoh, "This is the finger of God." But Pharaoh's heart was hardened, and he would not listen to them, as the Lord had said.

THE FOURTH PLAGUE: FLIES

[20] Then the Lord said to Moses, "Rise up early in the morning and present yourself to Pharaoh, as he goes out to the water, and say to him, 'Thus says the Lord, "Let my people go, that they may serve me. [21] Or else, if you will not let my people go, behold, I will send swarms of flies on you and your servants and your people, and into your houses. And the houses of the Egyptians shall be filled with swarms of flies, and also the ground on which they stand. [22] But on that day I will set apart the land of Goshen, where my people dwell, so that no swarms of flies shall be there, that you may know that I am the Lord in the midst of the earth. [23] Thus I will put a division between my people and your people. Tomorrow this sign shall happen."'" [24] And the Lord did so. There came great swarms of flies into the house of Pharaoh and into his servants' houses. Throughout all the land of Egypt the land was ruined by the swarms of flies.

²⁵ Then Pharaoh called Moses and Aaron and said, "Go, sacrifice to your God within the land." ²⁶ But Moses said, "It would not be right to do so, for the offerings we shall sacrifice to the LORD our God are an abomination to the Egyptians. If we sacrifice offerings abominable to the Egyptians before their eyes, will they not stone us? ²⁷ We must go three days' journey into the wilderness and sacrifice to the LORD our God as he tells us." ²⁸ So Pharaoh said, "I will let you go to sacrifice to the LORD your God in the wilderness; only you must not go very far away. Plead for me." ²⁹ Then Moses said, "Behold, I am going out from you and I will plead with the LORD that the swarms of flies may depart from Pharaoh, from his servants, and from his people, tomorrow. Only let not Pharaoh cheat again by not letting the people go to sacrifice to the LORD." ³⁰ So Moses went out from Pharaoh and prayed to the LORD. ³¹ And the LORD did as Moses asked, and removed the swarms of flies from Pharaoh, from his servants, and from his people; not one remained. ³² But Pharaoh hardened his heart this time also, and did not let the people go.

THE FIFTH PLAGUE: EGYPTIAN LIVESTOCK DIE

9 Then the LORD said to Moses, "Go in to Pharaoh and say to him, 'Thus says the LORD, the God of the Hebrews, "Let my people go, that they may serve me. ² For if you refuse to let them go and still hold them, ³ behold, the hand of the LORD will fall with a very severe plague upon your livestock that are in the field, the horses, the donkeys, the camels, the herds, and the flocks. ⁴ But the LORD will make a distinction between the livestock of Israel and the livestock of Egypt, so that nothing of all that belongs to the people of Israel shall die."'" ⁵ And the LORD set a time, saying, "Tomorrow the LORD will do this thing in the land." ⁶ And the next day the LORD did this thing. All the livestock of the Egyptians died, but not one of the livestock of the people of Israel died. ⁷ And Pharaoh sent, and behold, not one of the livestock of Israel was dead. But the heart of Pharaoh was hardened, and he did not let the people go.

THE SIXTH PLAGUE: BOILS

⁸ And the Lᴏʀᴅ said to Moses and Aaron, "Take handfuls of soot from the kiln, and let Moses throw them in the air in the sight of Pharaoh. ⁹ It shall become fine dust over all the land of Egypt, and become boils breaking out in sores on man and beast throughout all the land of Egypt." ¹⁰ So they took soot from the kiln and stood before Pharaoh. And Moses threw it in the air, and it became boils breaking out in sores on man and beast. ¹¹ And the magicians could not stand before Moses because of the boils, for the boils came upon the magicians and upon all the Egyptians. ¹² But the Lᴏʀᴅ hardened the heart of Pharaoh, and he did not listen to them, as the Lᴏʀᴅ had spoken to Moses.

THE SEVENTH PLAGUE: HAIL

¹³ Then the Lᴏʀᴅ said to Moses, "Rise up early in the morning and present yourself before Pharaoh and say to him, 'Thus says the Lᴏʀᴅ, the God of the Hebrews, "Let my people go, that they may serve me. ¹⁴ For this time I will send all my plagues on you yourself, and on your servants and your people, so that you may know that there is none like me in all the earth. ¹⁵ For by now I could have put out my hand and struck you and your people with pestilence, and you would have been cut off from the earth. ¹⁶ But for this purpose I have raised you up, to show you my power, so that my name may be proclaimed in all the earth. ¹⁷ You are still exalting yourself against my people and will not let them go. ¹⁸ Behold, about this time tomorrow I will cause very heavy hail to fall, such as never has been in Egypt from the day it was founded until now. ¹⁹ Now therefore send, get your livestock and all that you have in the field into safe shelter, for every man and beast that is in the field and is not brought home will die when the hail falls on them."'" ²⁰ Then whoever feared the word of the Lᴏʀᴅ among the servants of Pharaoh hurried his slaves and his

livestock into the houses, [21] but whoever did not pay attention to the word of the Lord left his slaves and his livestock in the field.

[22] Then the Lord said to Moses, "Stretch out your hand toward heaven, so that there may be hail in all the land of Egypt, on man and beast and every plant of the field, in the land of Egypt." [23] Then Moses stretched out his staff toward heaven, and the Lord sent thunder and hail, and fire ran down to the earth. And the Lord rained hail upon the land of Egypt. [24] There was hail and fire flashing continually in the midst of the hail, very heavy hail, such as had never been in all the land of Egypt since it became a nation. [25] The hail struck down everything that was in the field in all the land of Egypt, both man and beast. And the hail struck down every plant of the field and broke every tree of the field. [26] Only in the land of Goshen, where the people of Israel were, was there no hail.

[27] Then Pharaoh sent and called Moses and Aaron and said to them, "This time I have sinned; the Lord is in the right, and I and my people are in the wrong. [28] Plead with the Lord, for there has been enough of God's thunder and hail. I will let you go, and you shall stay no longer." [29] Moses said to him, "As soon as I have gone out of the city, I will stretch out my hands to the Lord. The thunder will cease, and there will be no more hail, so that you may know that the earth is the Lord's. [30] But as for you and your servants, I know that you do not yet fear the Lord God." [31] (The flax and the barley were struck down, for the barley was in the ear and the flax was in bud. [32] But the wheat and the emmer were not struck down, for they are late in coming up.) [33] So Moses went out of the city from Pharaoh and stretched out his hands to the Lord, and the thunder and the hail ceased, and the rain no longer poured upon the earth. [34] But when Pharaoh saw that the rain and the hail and the thunder had ceased, he sinned yet again and hardened his heart, he and

his servants. ³⁵ So the heart of Pharaoh was hardened, and he did not let the people of Israel go, just as the LORD had spoken through Moses.

THE EIGHTH PLAGUE: LOCUSTS

10 Then the LORD said to Moses, "Go in to Pharaoh, for I have hardened his heart and the heart of his servants, that I may show these signs of mine among them, ² and that you may tell in the hearing of your son and of your grandson how I have dealt harshly with the Egyptians and what signs I have done among them, that you may know that I am the LORD."

³ So Moses and Aaron went in to Pharaoh and said to him, "Thus says the LORD, the God of the Hebrews, 'How long will you refuse to humble yourself before me? Let my people go, that they may serve me. ⁴ For if you refuse to let my people go, behold, tomorrow I will bring locusts into your country, ⁵ and they shall cover the face of the land, so that no one can see the land. And they shall eat what is left to you after the hail, and they shall eat every tree of yours that grows in the field, ⁶ and they shall fill your houses and the houses of all your servants and of all the Egyptians, as neither your fathers nor your grandfathers have seen, from the day they came on earth to this day.'" Then he turned and went out from Pharaoh.

⁷ Then Pharaoh's servants said to him, "How long shall this man be a snare to us? Let the men go, that they may serve the LORD their God. Do you not yet understand that Egypt is ruined?" ⁸ So Moses and Aaron were brought back to Pharaoh. And he said to them, "Go, serve the LORD your God. But which ones are to go?" ⁹ Moses said, "We will go with our young and our old. We will go with our sons and daughters and with our flocks and herds, for we must hold a feast to the LORD." ¹⁰ But he said to them, "The LORD be with you, if ever I let you and your little ones go! Look, you have some evil purpose in mind. ¹¹ No! Go,

the men among you, and serve the LORD, for that is what you are asking." And they were driven out from Pharaoh's presence.

[12] Then the LORD said to Moses, "Stretch out your hand over the land of Egypt for the locusts, so that they may come upon the land of Egypt and eat every plant in the land, all that the hail has left." [13] So Moses stretched out his staff over the land of Egypt, and the LORD brought an east wind upon the land all that day and all that night. When it was morning, the east wind had brought the locusts. [14] The locusts came up over all the land of Egypt and settled on the whole country of Egypt, such a dense swarm of locusts as had never been before, nor ever will be again. [15] They covered the face of the whole land, so that the land was darkened, and they ate all the plants in the land and all the fruit of the trees that the hail had left. Not a green thing remained, neither tree nor plant of the field, through all the land of Egypt. [16] Then Pharaoh hastily called Moses and Aaron and said, "I have sinned against the LORD your God, and against you. [17] Now therefore, forgive my sin, please, only this once, and plead with the LORD your God only to remove this death from me." [18] So he went out from Pharaoh and pleaded with the LORD. [19] And the LORD turned the wind into a very strong west wind, which lifted the locusts and drove them into the Red Sea. Not a single locust was left in all the country of Egypt. [20] But the LORD hardened Pharaoh's heart, and he did not let the people of Israel go.

THE NINTH PLAGUE: DARKNESS

[21] Then the LORD said to Moses, "Stretch out your hand toward heaven, that there may be darkness over the land of Egypt, a darkness to be felt." [22] So Moses stretched out his hand toward heaven, and there was pitch darkness in all the land of Egypt three days. [23] They did not see one another, nor did anyone rise from his place for three days, but all

the people of Israel had light where they lived. 24 Then Pharaoh called Moses and said, "Go, serve the LORD; your little ones also may go with you; only let your flocks and your herds remain behind." 25 But Moses said, "You must also let us have sacrifices and burnt offerings, that we may sacrifice to the LORD our God. 26 Our livestock also must go with us; not a hoof shall be left behind, for we must take of them to serve the LORD our God, and we do not know with what we must serve the LORD until we arrive there." 27 But the LORD hardened Pharaoh's heart, and he would not let them go. 28 Then Pharaoh said to him, "Get away from me; take care never to see my face again, for on the day you see my face you shall die." 29 Moses said, "As you say! I will not see your face again."

1. OBSERVE: (question 3, p. 84) In Exodus 7:8-13, what happened when Moses and Aaron gave the sign that was intended to prove their authority from God?

APPLY: (question 4, p. 84) Have you ever asked God to give you a physical sign? Why should we trust the promises of God more than physical signs of His presence?

APPLY: (question 15, p. 87) When seeking to obey God, do we ever look for a compromise that covers most of what He requires instead of obeying completely? Give an example.

2. OBSERVE: (question 16, p. 88) Of the nine plague descriptions, how many contain a statement about the hardness of Pharaoh's heart?

APPLY: (question 18, p. 88) Have you ever made promises to God when you were in a crisis and then set them aside once the crisis had passed? Why do we tend to do this? What does this kind of behavior indicate we believe is true about God? About us?

3. OBSERVE: (question 20, p. 89) Do you see any significance to the order of the plagues? Why do you think God orders them as He does?

APPLY: (question 23, p. 90) Pharaoh was unwilling to give up his perceived right to keep the Israelites as his slaves. Even in the face of great opposition, he clung to his own will rather than submitting to the will of God. Is there a disobedient area of your heart that is hardened to the truth? What steps can you take to submit it to the softening power of the Holy Spirit?

4. WRAP-UP: (p. 90) What aspect of God's character has this week's passage of Exodus shown you more clearly?

Fill in the following statement:

Knowing that God is _____ **shows me that I am** _____ .

What one step can you take this week to better live in light of this truth?

WEEK SIX | VIEWER GUIDE NOTES

A Final Sign

Exodus 11:1–12:42

After nine plagues, a tenth and final plague will be sent on Egypt, a final pronouncement of the supremacy of God and a beautiful picture of salvation. Passover marks the climax of all that has happened thus far in the narrative. Moses emphasizes its significance by combining his narration of the historical event with instruction on how Israel will memorialize this pivotal moment "as a statute forever" (Ex. 12:14).

As you read this week, you may notice that the narrative seems to jump around from topic to topic. Chapter 11 sets the stage for the events and descriptions of chapter 12. Chapter 12 covers several topics in what seems to be no discernible order—moving from the institution of the Passover to the Feast of Unleavened Bread to the tenth plague, and then back to Passover.

To our untrained eyes, the text can be a little confusing. What you will read this week is actually part of an intentionally structured form of parallelism called a chiasmus. A chiasmus often builds to a central thought and then backs away from it in the order that it approached. This particular chiasmus stretches from Exodus 12:1 to 13:16. The summary statements below reveal its structure. Note how the central feature of the chiasmus is the exodus and the tenth plague:

A Instructions for preparing for plague on **firstborn** (12:1-13)

B Memorial of eating of unleavened **bread** (12:14-20)

C **Passover** meal instructions (12:21-28)

X Center: The exodus and tenth plague (12:29-42)

C' Additional **Passover** meal instructions (12:43-50)

B' Memorial of eating of unleavened **bread** (13:3-10)

A' Instructions for memorial of redeeming of **firstborn** (13:11-16)

READ EXODUS 11:1–12:42.

We will cover chapter 11 and the first four sections of the chiasmus this week, picking up with the last three sections in our Week Eight lesson. Write a two to three sentence summary for each of the divisions noted below:

1. Exodus 11

2. Exodus 12:1-20

3. Exodus 12:21-42

NOW LOOK BACK AT EXODUS 11:1-10.

4. What does God tell Moses that Pharaoh's response to the tenth and final plague will be (v. 1b)?

5. What instruction does God tell Moses to give to the people in preparation for the outcome of the tenth plague (v. 2)? Who is meant by the term *neighbor* (v. 2)?

6. How would you explain the fact that Moses was highly esteemed by the Egyptians (v. 3b)? Does this surprise you? Why or why not?

7. What are the first three words of verse 4?

    To whom is Moses describing the tenth plague (v. 8b)?

    Look back at Exodus 10:24-29. After the ninth plague, how does Moses' audience with Pharaoh end?

Why do you think we find an account of Moses addressing Pharaoh in hot anger in 11:4-8 after the account in 10:24-29? Check the answer that seems most likely:

_____ Pharaoh changed his mind and allowed Moses another audience to announce the tenth plague.

_____ The account is not chronological. Moses' words in 11:4-8 were spoken during his audience with Pharaoh after the ninth plague.

8. What is the nature of the tenth plague? Specifically, what will happen and who will be affected?

9. How is the nature of the tenth plague fitting? Look back at the following verses to help with your answer.

Exodus 1:22 | Exodus 4:22-23

10. What accounts for Moses' "hot anger" after his encounter with Pharaoh (11:8)? Do you think it is a sinful anger? Why or why not?

11. APPLY: Why did the Egyptian people react differently to Moses than Pharaoh did? (Compare 11:3b and 11:10.) How does pride keep us from recognizing the activity of God in our lives, even when others around us are seeing it?

NOW LOOK AT EXODUS 12:1-28.

As we noted earlier, chapter 12 tells of the departure from Egypt and the ritual feast set in place to remember it. The Feast of Unleavened Bread began with the Passover meal and continued for seven days after it. The feast and its observances are instituted in verses 1-28.

12. In our Week One introduction to the study, we noted that Moses wrote the first five books of the Bible (the Pentateuch) to give the Israelites "roots and shoots"—a history to remember as they looked back and a set of rules to guide them as they looked forward to life in the promised land. How do the descriptions and instructions in verses 1-28 support Moses' purpose in writing the Pentateuch?

13. Does it surprise you that more of chapter 12 is devoted to establishing the observance of Passover than to describing the tenth plague? Why or why not?

14. Note the details of the Passover feast below.

When it was to be observed (vv. 2-3,6)	

What was to be eaten
    Main dish (vv. 3-5)
    Side dishes (v. 8)	

How to prepare the meal (vv. 8-10)	
What ingredient to exclude (vv. 14-20)	
How to dress (v. 11)	
Where to place the blood of the lamb (v. 22)	
The purpose of the observance (vv. 12-13,23)	

15. The bitter herbs were to remind the Israelites of something. What was it? Look back at Exodus 1:13-14 and note what you find. Why would God want to regularly remind His people of this?

16. In the Bible, leaven (yeast) almost always symbolizes sin. How does this change your understanding of its treatment during Passover and the Feast of Unleavened Bread? How is leaven a good metaphor for sin?

17. APPLY: How frequently do you "clean house" with regard to the leaven of sin? Describe how believers can apply this spiritual metaphor today.

CONTINUE IN EXODUS 12:1-28.

18. What idea is repeated in both verse 14 and verse 17?

    ". . . you shall keep it [the Passover feast] as a feast to the LORD; throughout your generations, as a _____ _____ . . ." (v. 14, ESV).

    If this is the case, shouldn't Christians observe the feast of the Passover today? How does this feast still occur as an everlasting remembrance of deliverance from slavery? Look up the following verses in Matthew 26 and note what you find:

    Matthew 26:1-2

    Matthew 26:17-19

    Matthew 26:26-29

19. Next to each New Testament verse, note the connection that is established between Passover and the person and ministry of Christ:

    John 1:35-36

    1 Corinthians 5:7-8

    Colossians 1:18

    Hebrews 10:10-12

    1 Peter 1:18-20

    Revelation 5:6-14

20. APPLY: Consider the example of the angels and all living creatures in Revelation 5. How should believers of all ages respond to the fact that Jesus is our Passover Lamb?

21. What confident assertion about the future is made by God in Exodus 12:25?

Look up Isaiah 46:8-10. How does this beautiful passage teach us about the knowledge of God and reinforce the promise of Exodus 12:25?

22. APPLY: Though your current circumstance may be one of difficulty and uncertainty, what promises has the Lord given His children that are sure and true? What is the certain end of our journey? How should this knowledge impact the way we face our present circumstance?

NOW LOOK AT EXODUS 12:29-42.

23. What happens at midnight? Who is impacted?

24. How does Pharaoh respond to this final plague (vv. 31-32)? Does he negotiate as he has done in the past?

25. What is Pharaoh's final request of Moses when he summons him?
    ". . . and be gone, and _____ _____ _____!" (v. 32b, ESV).

    Compare this statement to Exodus 5:1-2. What were his first words to Moses?

26. Was Pharaoh the only one in a hurry to see the Israelites depart (12:33)?

27. What did the Israelites carry, in addition to their unleavened bread (vv. 35-36)? Why do you think God allowed the Israelites to plunder the wealth of the Egyptians?

28. How many Israelite men were said to have left Egypt in the Exodus (v. 37)?

    Look back at Week Two of your homework, question 5, on page 19. How many people were recorded as having gone into Egypt to escape the famine?

29. APPLY: What do these numbers tell you about the faithfulness of God to the people of God?

30. How many years were the people of Israel in Egypt (v. 40)?

Why do you think the Lord allowed His people to live in slavery for so long?

31. Look at verse 42. How would you paraphrase what Moses is saying?

32. APPLY: The Lord has kept watch over you. In the dark night of judgment, He has kept watch over you and preserved your life by the blood of His Son. How can you respond with watchfulness? Look up the following verses and reflect on how you can practice watchfulness in remembrance of what God has done for you. What hinders watchfulness? What helps it?

Matthew 26:41

Luke 12:35-40

1 Timothy 4:16

Did you see evidence of the theme of deliverance in this week's passage?
If so, where?

What aspect of God's character has this week's passage of Exodus shown you
more clearly?

Fill in the following statement:

Knowing that God is   **shows me that
I am**   **.**

What one step can you take this week to better live in light of this truth?

WEEK SEVEN | GROUP DISCUSSION

1. **OBSERVE:** (question 5, p. 107) What instruction does God tell Moses to give to the people in preparation for the outcome of the tenth plague (Ex. 11:2)? Who is meant by the term *neighbor* (v. 2)?

   APPLY: (question 11, p. 108) Why did the Egyptian people react differently to Moses than Pharaoh did? (Compare Ex. 11:3b and 11:10.) How does pride keep us from recognizing the activity of God in our lives, even when others around us are seeing it?

2. **OBSERVE:** (question 18, p. 111) What idea is repeated in both Exodus 12:14 and 12:17?

   ". . . you shall keep it [the Passover feast] as a feast to the LORD; throughout your generations, as a _____ _____ . . ." (ESV).

   APPLY: (question 20, p. 112) Consider the example of the angels and all living creatures in Revelation 5. How should believers of all ages respond to the fact that Jesus is our Passover Lamb?

3. **OBSERVE:** (question 21, p. 112) What confident assertion about the future was made by God in Exodus 12:25? Look up Isaiah 46:8-10. How does this beautiful passage teach us about the knowledge of God and reinforce the promise of Exodus 12:25?

   APPLY: (question 22, p. 112) Though your current circumstance may be one of difficulty and uncertainty, what promises has the Lord given His children that are sure and true? What is the certain end of our journey? How should this knowledge impact the way we face our present circumstance?

4. **OBSERVE:** (question 28, p. 113) How many Israelite men were said to have left Egypt in the Exodus (Ex. 12:37)? Look back at Week Two of your homework, question 5, on page 19. How many people were recorded as having gone into Egypt to escape the famine?

APPLY: (question 29, p. 114) What do these numbers tell you about the faithfulness of God to the people of God?

APPLY: (question 32, p. 114) The Lord has kept watch over you. In the dark night of judgment, He has kept watch over you and preserved your life by the blood of His Son. How can you respond with watchfulness? Look up the following verses and reflect on how you can practice watchfulness in remembrance of what God has done for you. What hinders watchfulness? What helps it?

Matthew 26:41

Luke 12:35-40

1 Timothy 4:16

5. WRAP-UP: (p. 115) What aspect of God's character has this week's passage of Exodus shown you more clearly?

Fill in the following statement:

Knowing that God is _____ **shows me that I am** _____ .

What one step can you take this week to better live in light of this truth?

A People Called Out

Exodus 12:43–15:21

Having fled Egypt with the wealth of the Egyptians and the clothing on their backs, the Israelites begin their trek to Mount Sinai. But a seemingly broken Pharaoh is about to demonstrate the full extent of the hardness of his heart.

READ EXODUS 12:43–15:21.

1. Summarize 12:43–13:22 in two to three sentences.

2. Summarize 14:1–15:21 in two to three sentences.

3. What is the tone at the end of this week's section of the story?

NOW LOOK BACK AT EXODUS 12:43-51.

You may remember from last week's lesson that the end of chapter 12 and the beginning of chapter 13 complete the chiasmatic parallel focused on the exodus of the Israelites from Egypt. Moses revisited the topics of the Passover and the Feast of Unleavened Bread before resuming with the narrative of what happened next to Israel.

4. In verses 43-49, who does the Lord say may partake of the Passover meal?

    Who must not partake of it?

    Based on what the meal commemorates, how does this make sense?

5. How do the restrictions on who may partake of the Passover meal parallel restrictions on who may partake of the Lord's Supper? Who would a "foreigner" be with regard to the Lord's Supper?

6. What further picture of the future work of Christ is given to us in verse 46? Look up the following verses and note what you find:

    Psalm 34:19-20

    John 19:31-36

NOW LOOK AT EXODUS 13:1-16.

7. In memorial of the death of the firstborn of Egypt (v. 15), what was to be consecrated to the Lord (v. 2)?

8. What does it mean to *consecrate* something or someone? Look up the word *consecrate* in a dictionary and write a definition for it below that fits the context of verses 1-2.

9. In Numbers 3:11-13 God chooses another group to be consecrated to His service in place of the firstborn of Israel. Who is that group?

10. Look at Exodus 13:8,14. Look back at 12:26-27 as well. What common thought do they contain?

    Now look up Psalm 78. Take time to read the entire psalm. Then look specifically at verse 7. What reason is given for telling the next generation of God's past faithfulness?

11. APPLY: How deliberate are you about telling the next generation about your reasons for belief and obedience? How could you be more deliberate?

NOW LOOK AT EXODUS 13:17–14:4.

12. What reason is given in 13:17 for not taking the direct route to the Land of Canaan?

    Do the Israelites lack weapons (13:18)?

    ___ Yes ___ No

    What do you think the Israelites would have lacked in a battle confrontation at this time?

13. What visible form does the Lord take to lead the Israelites (13:21-22)? Why do you think this was so?

14. In 14:1-3, why does God tell Moses to encamp in an area where, from a military standpoint, they are trapped? How would obedience to make camp in that spot ultimately glorify God?

15. APPLY: Based on how you answered the previous question, what truth can you focus on when you feel trapped in a circumstance or relationship?

16. On the next page is a map showing a commonly accepted route of the exodus as the bold broken line leading out of the Land of Goshen. By the end of this study, Israel will have traveled to the foot of Mount Sinai, only a small part of her journey to the promised land.

- Highlight the route of the exodus on the map below.

- Circle Mount Sinai on the map.

- The location of Succoth is uncertain. Mark on the map where Israel encamped, according to 14:2.

- Circle the location of Canaan (the promised land) in the upper right-hand corner of the map between the Great Sea and the Dead Sea.

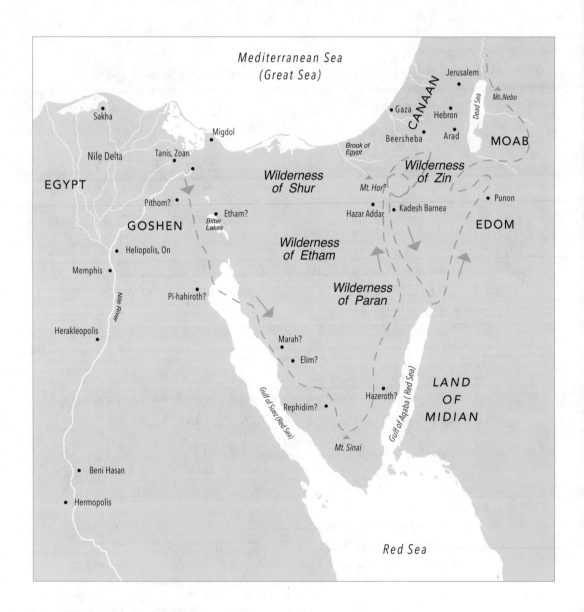

17. Clearly, the Israelites are taking the "scenic route" to the land of Canaan. Note that they have yet to disobey the Lord. What purpose do you think God had in taking His newly-birthed nation on a journey that appears much longer than necessary?

18. APPLY: Have you ever been taken on the "scenic route" by God before seeing His promises fulfilled? How would your understanding of His character and promises have been different if He had taken you by the shortest route?

Map Sources

1. "The Route of the Exodus," *CSB Study Bible* (Nashville, TN: Holman Bible Publishers, 2017).

2. "Pi-hahiroth," *BibleHub*, accessed February 4, 2021, https://bibleatlas.org/full/pi-hahiroth.htm.

NOW LOOK AT EXODUS 14:5-31.

19. What happens once Pharaoh had time to reflect on the fact that his slaves had all left (vv. 5-9)?

20. How many of his army does he take in pursuit of the Israelites (vv. 6-7,9)?

21. What is the response of the Israelites to seeing the entire Egyptian army coming after them? Paraphrase their words found in verses 11-12:

22. Paraphrase Moses' response to the people in verses 13-14. Note specifically what the role of the Israelites needs to be in this crisis (v. 14b).

23. In two to three sentences, summarize what happens in verses 19-29.

24. What is the outcome of the Red Sea crossing? Note below everything the Israelites see and believe (vv. 30-31).

25. We often say that "seeing is believing." This was certainly true of Israel and is true of us as well. Read John 20:24-29. What form of belief does Jesus pronounce a blessing on?

26. APPLY: What unseen truth is it hardest for you to believe right now? How might exercising faith in that area result in blessing?

NOW READ EXODUS 15:1-21.

27. The Song of Moses divides into two sections, with a transition verse in the middle (v. 13). Next to the section reference below, summarize what its message is and what picture it paints of God:

    Verses 1-12

    • Message:

    • Picture of God:

    Verses 14-18

    • Message:

    • Picture of God:

28. How is God described in verses 3 and 12? Look up the description of Him in Isaiah 59:16-18 and note how it expands on His warlike nature. How does the Lord dress for battle?

29. Whose hand has Israel learned to celebrate in Exodus 15:6?

    Note how many times the hand of God is mentioned in the Song of Moses:

    Whose celebration is specifically noted in verses 20-21?
    ". . . _____ the _____, the _____ of _____"
    (v. 20, ESV).

    Who is Miriam's other brother?

In what other instance did she likely celebrate the safe passage through the waters of someone facing certain death at the hands of Pharaoh? Look back at Exodus 2:4,7 to help with your answer.

30. APPLY: Miriam celebrates because she has seen the great faithfulness of God to protect and deliver. Have you seen that same faithfulness? How can you remember and celebrate publicly what the Lord has done for you?

WRAP-UP

Did you see evidence of the theme of deliverance in this week's passage? If so, where?

What aspect of God's character has this week's passage of Exodus shown you more clearly?

Fill in the following statement:

Knowing that God is   **shows me that I am**   .

What one step can you take this week to better live in light of this truth?

1. **OBSERVE:** (question 8, p. 124) What does it mean to *consecrate* something or someone? Look up the word *consecrate* in a dictionary and write a definition for it that fits the context of Exodus 13:1-2.

   APPLY: (question 11, p. 124) How deliberate are you about telling the next generation about your reasons for belief and obedience? How could you be more deliberate?

2. **OBSERVE:** (question 14, p. 125) In Exodus 14:1-3, why does God tell Moses to encamp in an area where, from a military standpoint, they are trapped? How would obedience to make camp in that spot ultimately glorify God?

   APPLY: (question 15, p. 125) Based on how you answered the previous question, what truth can you focus on when you feel trapped in a circumstance or relationship?

3. **OBSERVE:** (question 17, p. 127) Clearly, the Israelites are taking the "scenic route" to the land of Canaan. Note that they had yet to disobey the Lord. What purpose do you think God had in taking his newly-birthed nation on a journey that appears much longer than necessary?

   APPLY: (question 18, p. 127) Have you ever been taken on the "scenic route" by God before seeing His promises fulfilled? How would your understanding of His character and promises have been different if He had taken you by the shortest route?

4. **OBSERVE:** (question 25, p. 129) We often say that "seeing is believing." This was certainly true of Israel and is true of us as well. Read John 20:24-29. What form of belief does Jesus pronounce a blessing on?

   APPLY: (question 26, p. 129) What unseen truth is it hardest for you to believe right now? How might exercising faith in that area result in blessing?

5. OBSERVE: (question 28, p. 130) How is God described in Exodus 15:3,12? Look up the description of Him in Isaiah 59:16-18 and note how it expands on His warlike nature. How does the Lord dress for battle?

APPLY: (question 30, p. 131) Miriam celebrates because she has seen the great faithfulness of God to protect and deliver. Have you seen that same faithfulness? How can you remember and celebrate publicly what the Lord has done for you?

6. WRAP-UP: (p. 131) What aspect of God's character has this week's passage of Exodus shown you more clearly?

Fill in the following statement:

Knowing that God is _____ **shows me that I am** _____ .

What one step can you take this week to better live in light of this truth?

WEEK EIGHT | VIEWER GUIDE NOTES

Provision from Heaven

Exodus 15:22–16:36

With a miraculous deliverance in their immediate past and the songs of celebration still ringing in their thoughts, the Israelites set out into the wilderness. They are finally free. But freedom in the wilderness will test their expectations and their trust of God in a thousand new ways.

READ EXODUS 15:22–16:36.

1. Summarize 15:22-27 in one to two sentences.

2. Summarize chapter 16 in two to three sentences.

3. Choose one word to describe each of the following characters in this week's section:

    The Israelites

    Moses

    God

NOW LOOK BACK AT EXODUS 15:22-27.

4. What two stops do the Israelites make in this passage?

    Verse 23

    Verse 27

    Look back at your map from last week on page 126. Draw a circle around these two locations.

5. How long are the Israelites in the wilderness before they come to Marah?

6. To whom do the Israelites voice their complaint about the travel conditions (v. 24)?

    What attitude do you think is behind their grumbling?

7. How does the Lord respond to Moses' request on behalf of His grumbling people (v. 25)?

8. Not far from Marah was Elim, a place of provision and comfort, a literal oasis. Before arriving there, why does God first bring His thirsty people to Marah?
    ". . . and there he _____ them" *(v. 25b, ESV).*

9. What is the nature of the test? Think back to the first plague God brought upon Egypt (Ex. 7:19) and then look at the Lord's words in Exodus 12:26-27.

    Do the Israelites pass the test? Explain your answer.

10. What name does the Lord give for Himself in Exodus 15:26b? What fear does He want to address?

11. APPLY: Are you ever impatient for the Lord's provision? To whom do you grumble in those times? What would be a better way to "diligently listen to the voice of the LORD . . . and do that which is right in his eyes" (v. 26a) when facing unexpected difficulty?

DAY THREE

NOW LOOK AT EXODUS 16:1-21.

12. On your map on page 126, label the Wilderness of Sin based on the location given for it in verse 1.

13. Approximately how many days have the Israelites been travelling thus far (v. 1)?

14. To whom do the Israelites voice their complaint about the travel conditions (v. 2)?

    Paraphrase their complaint in verse 3:

15. What do Moses and Aaron tell the people about their grumbling in verses 6-9?

    What is the tone of their statement? Check the most accurate answer below. Explain why you chose it.
    _____ tolerant   _____ generous   _____ cautionary

16. What two food items does God provide for His people (vv. 13-15)?

    _____ and _____

    How are these two items a direct response to the grumblings of the people (v. 3)?

17. What unit of measurement is used for gathering the bread God sent from heaven (vv. 16-17)?

An _____

An omer (some translations say "two quarts") was the equivalent of what one person needed to be fed for one day. What happened if the people tried to gather more than what they needed for that day (vv. 19-20)?

18. What principle is God illustrating for His people with the bread from heaven? Look up the following words of Jesus to help with your answer:

Matthew 6:9-11 | Matthew 6:25-34

19. APPLY: How hard is it for you to trust God to provide daily bread? What aspect of tomorrow are you commonly anxious about? How is the story of manna and quail a reassurance to you? How does it challenge you?

NOW LOOK AT EXODUS 16:22-30.

20. Why is there no bread to gather on the seventh day? Look up the following verses to help with your answer:

Genesis 2:1-3 | Exodus 20:8-11

21. How does God intend the Sabbath day to be used?
As a day of _____

Is the Sabbath intended as a restriction or as a gift? Explain your answer.

22. What does the fact that the Israelites go out to gather on the seventh day, even though they have sufficient bread already, reveal about their hearts?

23. APPLY: How are we like Israel? What wrong beliefs about our own efforts rob us of the rest God commands and graciously provides? What activities are hardest for us to set aside when it is time to rest?

NOW LOOK AT EXODUS 16:31-36.

24. What does God command to be done with some of the manna?

What is the purpose of this command (v. 32b)?

"... *so that they may* _____ _____ _____ *with which I fed you in the wilderness . . . " (ESV).*

25. Look at verses 33-34. Where was the jar of manna to be placed? Look up Hebrews 9:2-4 to further clarify this location.

26. How is the promised land described in Exodus 16:35?
    "*a* _____ *land" (ESV).*

By contrast, what kind of land is the wilderness? In a dictionary, look up the word you wrote above and write a definition for its antonym (opposite) below.

27. If the Lord had not provided manna and quail in the wilderness for the people of Israel, what would have been their fate? What do you think Israel was to learn and remember from this provision?

28. God allows His people to experience thirst before giving them water and hunger before giving them bread. Why do you think this was so?

29. APPLY: What physical lack are you currently experiencing? How might God use it to point you toward a deeper dependence on Him?

What spiritual lack are you currently experiencing? How might God use it to point you toward a deeper dependence on Him?

WRAP-UP

Did you see evidence of the theme of deliverance in this week's passage? If so, where?

What aspect of God's character has this week's passage of Exodus shown you more clearly?

Fill in the following statement:

Knowing that God is _____ shows me that I am _____.

What one step can you take this week to better live in light of this truth?

NOTES

1. **OBSERVE:** (question 7, p. 139) How does the Lord respond to Moses' request on behalf of His grumbling people (Ex. 15:25)?

   APPLY: (question 11, p. 140) Are you ever impatient for the Lord's provision? To whom do you grumble in those times? What would be a better way to "diligently listen to the voice of the LORD . . . and do that which is right in his eyes" (Ex. 15:26a) when facing unexpected difficulty?

2. **OBSERVE:** (question 18, p. 142) What principle is God illustrating for His people with the bread from heaven? Look up the following words of Jesus to help with your answer:
   Matthew 6:9-11 | Matthew 6:25-34

   APPLY: (question 19, p. 142) How hard is it for you to trust God to provide daily bread? What aspect of tomorrow are you commonly anxious about? How is the story of manna and quail a reassurance to you? How does it challenge you?

3. **OBSERVE:** (question 21, p. 143) How did God intend the Sabbath day to be used? As a day of _____
   Is the Sabbath intended as a restriction or as a gift? Explain your answer.

   APPLY: (question 23, p. 143) How are we like Israel? What wrong beliefs about our own efforts rob us of the rest God commands and graciously provides? What activities are hardest for us to set aside when it is time to rest?

4. **OBSERVE:** (question 28, p. 145) God allows His people to experience thirst before giving them water and hunger before giving them bread. Why do you think this was so?

APPLY: (question 29, p. 145) What physical lack are you currently experiencing? How might God use it to point you toward a deeper dependence on Him? What spiritual lack are you currently experiencing? How might God use it to point you toward a deeper dependence on Him?

5. WRAP-UP: (p. 146) What aspect of God's character has this week's passage of Exodus shown you more clearly?

Fill in the following statement:

Knowing that God is _____ **shows me that I am** _____ .

What one step can you take this week to better live in light of this truth?

WEEK NINE | VIEWER GUIDE NOTES

To Sinai

Exodus 17–18

Having been shown the Lord's rich provision for their thirst, their hunger, and their rest, the Israelites journey on toward the foot of Mount Sinai. But further challenges await them along the way.

READ EXODUS 17–18.

1. Summarize chapter 17 in two to three sentences.

2. Summarize chapter 18 in two to three sentences.

NOW LOOK BACK AT EXODUS 17:1-7.

3. Where do the Israelites make camp after their time in the Wilderness of Sin (v. 1)?

   Look back at your map from last week on page 126. Draw a circle around this location.

4. What problem confronts Israel at Rephidim?

   What is their response? Is it the same as at Marah and the Wilderness of Sin? Read through verses 2-4 and note any clues that support your answer.

5. In verses 5-6, we read the instructions God gives to Moses and Moses' response. What did God tell Moses to do?

   Why do you think Moses is to use the staff? What does the staff symbolize?

   Specifically, what group is Moses told to gather as witnesses of this miracle? Why do you think this is so?

6. Look up 1 Corinthians 10:1-4. How does this passage add to your understanding of the story of Moses striking the rock at Horeb? What does the story point toward?

7. Moses names the location of this particular test with two names. What are they (Ex. 17:7)? What does each name mean? *(Hint: check the footnote in your Bible.)*

8. At Marah, who tested whom (15:25b)?

   At Rephidim, who tested whom (17:7)?

   Look up Deuteronomy 6:16-17. Why is it acceptable for God to test us but not for us to test God?

9. APPLY: Have you ever put God to the test by saying "If you do X, then I will do Y" or by asking Him to prove He is who He has promised to be? What was the outcome? What sinful motive was behind your desire to test God?

10. APPLY: Have you ever had a quarreling spirit toward God? What is the difference between the person who faces difficulty with grumbling and the one who faces it with a quiet spirit?

NOW LOOK AT EXODUS 17:8-16.

11. The Amalekites were a group of Bedouin tribes that inhabited the desert to the south of Canaan. Why do you think they would attack the Israelites unprovoked? What was their most likely objective?

12. Look up Deuteronomy 25:17-18. How does this later account of the battle add to your understanding of Amalek's strategy? Did Amalek fight fair?

13. What is the source of Israel's victory over Amalek in Exodus 17? is it a divine victory or a human victory? Explain your answer.

14. In what way does each of the following contribute to the outcome of the battle?

    Moses

    Aaron and Hur

    Joshua

    God

15. What do we learn about Moses' character in verses 8-13?

16. What is Moses instructed to write down and recite "in the ears of Joshua" (v. 14)?

Why do you think this instruction is given? Why would Joshua benefit from this?

17. What does Moses do in response to Israel's victory over the Amalekites (v. 15)?

What does he name the altar (v. 15)?

What is the altar's purpose? Check all that apply:
____ to offer sacrifice of thanksgiving
____ to serve as a memorial to God's faithfulness
____ to establish ownership of land

18. In your own words, explain what you think is meant by the name Moses gives the altar. Consider the purpose of a banner in battle. Look up Psalm 60:4 to help you with your answer.

19. APPLY: In what way has the Lord been your banner in times of unprovoked conflict? How can you "build an altar" to those times?

NOW LOOK AT EXODUS 18:1-12.

20. Which of Moses' family members reenters the narrative in this section (vv. 1-5)?

21. We already know of Moses' firstborn son, Gershom, from earlier in the narrative (Ex. 2:22). Where was Moses living when he was born?

    During what time of Moses' life would you guess his second son, Eliezer, was born?

    What does the name Eliezer mean (Ex. 18:4)? How is it a doubly fitting name for the son of Moses?

22. Why might Moses have sent away his family while trying to convince Pharaoh to let Israel go?

23. What kind of a greeting is described in verses 7-9? What do you learn about the relationship between Moses and his father-in-law Jethro?

24. Summarize Jethro's words and actions in verses 10-12.

Verse 10

Verse 11

Verse 12

What do his words and actions reveal about the state of his heart toward the God of Israel?

25. APPLY: Sacrifice was a part of Israel's observance marking both war (Ex. 17:15) and peace (18:12). Does worship mark many areas of your life or just some? How could you more faithfully practice worship when things are hard? When things are easy?

NOW LOOK AT EXODUS 18:13-27.

26. What aspect of Moses' character do we see in verses 13-16?

27. Summarize Moses' strategy for administering justice and settling disputes.

28. Moses clearly has a gift for sound judgment. What is he less gifted at (vv. 17-18)?

29. What solution does Jethro propose to help Moses in leadership (vv. 19-23)? Summarize his leadership strategy.

30. How is Jethro's advice not only wise counsel for Moses but also great help for the Israelites? How would it benefit them?

31. Look closer at verse 21. What leadership qualities are given here?

What qualities do we tend to look for in Christian leaders? How does what we often look for compare with this list? Explain your answer.

32. How does Moses respond to his father-in-law's advice (v. 24)? What does his response reveal about his character?

33. APPLY: When you are given advice that addresses an area of weakness, how do you respond? How is Moses an example to you?

34. How is the story of the battle with Amalek in chapter 17 similar to the story of Moses and Jethro in chapter 18? What common theme do these stories emphasize?

35. APPLY: How do your words and actions support the leadership of your church? Are you characterized by grumbling or by undergirding? How can you help lighten their load?

WRAP-UP

Did you see evidence of the theme of deliverance in this week's passage?
If so, where?

What aspect of God's character has this week's passage of Exodus shown you
more clearly?

Fill in the following statement:

Knowing that God is   **shows me that
I am**   .

What one step can you take this week to better live in light of this truth?

1. **OBSERVE:** (question 8, p. 156) At Marah, who tested whom (Ex. 15:25b)? At Rephidim, who tested whom (17:7)? Look up Deuteronomy 6:16-17. Why is it acceptable for God to test us but not for us to test God?

   APPLY: (question 9, p. 156) Have you ever put God to the test by saying "If you do X, then I will do Y" or by asking Him to prove He is who He has promised to be? What was the outcome? What sinful motive was behind your desire to test God?

   APPLY: (question 10, p. 156) Have you ever had a quarreling spirit toward God? What is the difference between the person who faces difficulty with grumbling and the one who faces it with a quiet spirit?

2. **OBSERVE:** (question 18, p. 158) In your own words, explain what you think is meant by the name Moses gives the altar. Consider the purpose of a banner in battle. Look up Psalm 60:4 to help you with your answer.

   APPLY: (question 19, p. 158) In what way has the Lord been your banner in times of unprovoked conflict? How can you "build an altar" to those times?

3. **OBSERVE:** (question 23, p. 159) What kind of a greeting is described in Exodus 18:7-9? What do you learn about the relationship between Moses and his father-in-law Jethro?

   APPLY: (question 25, p. 160) Sacrifice was a part of Israel's observance marking both war (Ex. 17:15) and peace (18:12). Does worship mark many areas of your life or just some? How could you more faithfully practice worship when things are hard? When things are easy?

4. **OBSERVE:** (question 29, p. 161) What solution does Jethro propose to help Moses in leadership (Ex. 18:19-23)? Summarize his leadership strategy.

APPLY: (question 33, p. 162) When you are given advice that addresses an area of weakness, how do you respond? How is Moses an example to you?

5. OBSERVE: (question 34, p. 162) How is the story of the battle with Amalek in chapter 17 similar to the story of Moses and Jethro in chapter 18? What common theme do these stories emphasize?

APPLY: (question 35, p. 162) How do your words and actions support the leadership of your church? Are you characterized by grumbling or by undergirding? How can you help lighten their load?

6. WRAP-UP: (p. 163) What aspect of God's character has this week's passage of Exodus shown you more clearly?

Fill in the following statement:

Knowing that God is _____ **shows me that I am** _____ .

What one step can you take this week to better live in light of this truth?

WEEK TEN | VIEWER GUIDE NOTES

Wrap-up

Congratulations! You made it to the foot of Mount Sinai after ten weeks of walking faithfully through the first part of Exodus. Now is the time to reflect on what you've learned so far, taking comprehension, interpretation, and application of the text out into the world.

The following is an optional wrap-up session to help you process what you've learned and live in light of who God is—One who sees, hears, and acts on the behalf of His people, the One who delivers.

1. What one image, idea, or story will you remember the most from the first eighteen chapters of Exodus? Why?

2. We have made it our challenge during the course of this study to look for Christ in the words of Moses (John 5:46-47). Reflect on the ground we have covered and note below as many instances as you can recall that we found Him there.

   In the story of Moses' childhood

   In the unique ministry of Moses to the people of Israel

   In the story of the plagues

   In the story of Passover and the Exodus

   In the story of the journey to Mount Sinai

3. Exodus is a book about deliverance. Having studied the first half, how has your understanding of your own personal deliverance from the bondage of sin changed?

Close in prayer. Thank God that from the earliest pages of His Word, deliverance was clearly in His view. Ask Him to give you eyes to see how the words of Exodus inform and enrich the words of the rest of Scripture. Confess your great need of Him, of deliverance from the bondage of sin. Thank Him that provision has been made for your need in the person of Christ, the Lamb of God, the Living Water, the Bread of Life, the Rock of Ages.

APPENDIX: THE ATTRIBUTES OF GOD

Attentive: God hears and responds to the needs of His children.

Compassionate: God cares for His children and acts on their behalf.

Creator: God made everything. He is uncreated.

Deliverer: God rescues and saves His children.

Eternal: God is not limited by time; He exists outside of time.

Faithful: God always keeps His promises.

Generous: God gives what is best and beyond what is deserved.

Glorious: God displays His greatness and worth.

Good: God is what is best and gives what is best. He is incapable of doing harm.

Holy: God is perfect, pure, and without sin.

Immutable/Unchanging: God never changes. He is the same yesterday, today, and tomorrow.

Incomprehensible: God is beyond our understanding. We can comprehend Him in part but not in whole.

Infinite: God has no limits in His person or on His power.

Jealous: God will not share His glory with another. All glory rightfully belongs to Him.

Just: God is fair in all His actions and judgments. He cannot over-punish or under-punish.

Loving: God feels and displays infinite, unconditional affection toward His children. His love for them does not depend on their worth, response, or merit.

Merciful: God does not give His children the punishment they deserve.